TORVILL AND DEAN

F*I*R*E O*N I*C*E

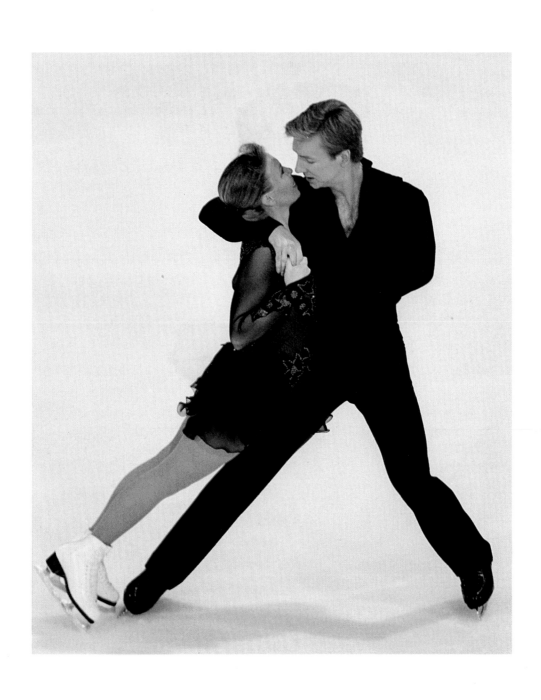

TORVILL AND DEAN

F*I*R*E O*N I*C*E

JAYNE TORVILL AND CHRISTOPHER DEAN
WITH NEIL WILSON
PHOTOGRAPHS BY BOB MARTIN

Weidenfeld and Nicolson
London

P*R*E*F*A*C*E

During the last few weeks, the question everybody has asked has been why we chose to pit ourselves again against the best amateur ice dancers in the world. Were our achievements before, all the medals and the acclaim, not enough for any two people in one lifetime?

The answer is, simply, the challenge. It is that which has been behind everything we have ever done, whether it was amateur sport, professional competitions or commercial shows. It is what has driven us, what has made it all worthwhile. And what bigger challenge could there have been than coming back into the Olympic arena ten years after we walked out of it for what we thought would be the last time?

For years we have enjoyed artistic freedom, a licence denied those in most sports. We could skate to our hearts' content. We were our own bosses. We could rehearse when we wanted, where we wanted. Any music, any dance, just as long as it pleased us and an audience.

Now we're restricted again. There are rules we must follow, areas we cannot enter. Before we do anything, we have to ask our trainers Betty Callaway and Bobby Thompson whether it is allowed. And, worst of all, there is getting up in the morning again before seven to drive a long way to

THE COMEBACK
We decided to return to our roots. We took advantage of an invitation to professional skaters from the International Skating Union to return to our competitions, and prepared for one more season. Our first amateur performance after ten years was at the British Championships in Sheffield in January 1994.

A LOVE STORY
With the melodramtic
love story of Mack
Sennett and Mabel
Normand we managed
to reach a public
beyond ice dancing,
even though the
Broadway show from
which we borrowed
the idea bombed and
was pulled off after
nine days.

a public rink that is willing to give us the time to practise before it opens its doors to the public.

No matter what the results, the challenge has been worth it: it is an adventure. New music to be chosen, new steps to be choreographed and learned, new costumes to be designed and made. A new role to be played.

Life is too short to be still. We've been asked a thousand times since Sarajevo to dance Bolero, or Barnum, or Mack and Mabel. But our favourite routine, our favourite piece of music, is always the one we are working on at the time. That's the challenge.

How do we come up with the routines? Usually when we're not thinking about it. Most of the music we have used has been heard when we were not looking for anything, and it stuck in our minds. Let's Face the Music and Dance, which we used this winter as our free programme, was an idea ages before we thought about trying for the Olympics again.

This book covers our skating lives from the early days, and there are pictures within it we're embarrassed to look at now. But they are a part of the story, part of what we are and what we have done. They bring back memories. We hope they will for you.

T·O·R·V·I·L·L

A·N·D

D·E·A·N

Torvill and Dean. Two names for one word in the mind of anyone who has ever seen them perform. A brand name for perfection. It has become a cliché, a word for the sublime blend of artistry to which every journalist and commentator retreats as the only description worthy of the performances, sporting or theatrical, that an extraordinary couple from Nottingham have given the world. Their names, wrote one admirer, go together like love and marriage, but those can be separable; you could have one without the other. But Torvill and Dean are one, two names so indivisible in the public mind that you can't imagine one without the other.

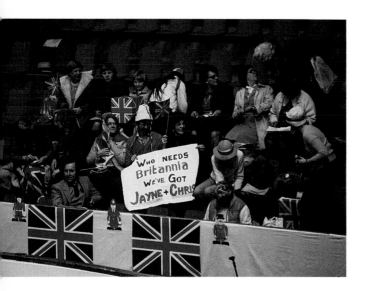

A VITAL PART OF THE TEAM
The British fans were a continual source of support for us. Without the enthusiasm they displayed over the years, we never could have achieved what we did.

INSPIRATION
Barnum was an idea that came to Chris as he watched the Moscow State Circus. He had swapped a ticket for the Bolshoi Ballet with another skater.

There was a time, of course, when their names weren't heard outside an inner-city ice rink in Nottingham, but now it would be enough in the British Isles to talk of Jayne and Chris for introductions to be unnecessary. Even beyond their native land they are known, probably because they have drawn admiring crowds in places where the only ice clinks in glasses.

Torvill and Dean are everywhere synonymous with a degree of excellence so rare that it is hard to think of its like. Rolls and Royce, perhaps. Astaire and Rogers, Fonteyn and Nureyev? All are so immaculately matched and so finely in tune with each other that they have reached heights that are the stuff of legend.

Whether what Torvill and Dean did was ever merely sport has been the cause of much debate. That they extended the concept of sporting competition far beyond the common boundaries of the arena is unquestionable; they painted indelible pictures in the mind's eye that will linger long after the results are forgotten.

Their record as sporting competitors speaks for itself. Pure gold. In their earlier incarnation, they won six British championships, three European and four world titles, and on a magical evening in Sarajevo in the former republic of Yugoslavia they were crowned Olympic champions.

'The greatest ice dancers ever', was the opinion of

Lawrence Demmy, himself a former world champion, who was to become the sport's foremost international official. Statistically, his statement cannot be in dispute. They achieved a standard unlikely ever to be equalled. Maximum scores of sixes in every element of the sport, more than a hundred and fifty during their career. In the Olympic free-dance programme in Sarajevo they were awarded the highest score recorded in the sport of figure skating: 107.4 out of a possible total of 108 – a world record that still stands today.

So great were their sporting achievements that they came to transcend sport. BBC Television's Nine O'Clock News, an institution, was rescheduled to accommodate their performances, as was the printing of newspapers. They were honoured in the highest quarters, with MBEs by the Queen at Buckingham Palace and receptions at 10 Downing Street. Recently they were also given honorary Master of Arts degrees from Nottingham Trent University. T & D entered the language as an acronym.

But sport was limiting to them. The rules and restrictions that are a necessary element of all competition was frustrating. They had stretched the rules where they could – a lift here, a flip-over there – but there was only so much that could be achieved within the four minutes the sport allowed them. Dean, the great innovator, wanted more.

While the sporting world was still buzzing with the beauty of Bolero, they finally took their leave and set off on another challenging journey as professional performers, innovators still, but in the broader arena where applause and the box office are the final arbiters of success.

Now they are back, challenged by a rule change to become competitors again on the Olympic stage, and it is as if noth-

ing has changed. The years just fell away; the decade disap-
peared as if a single moment. They are as good as ever, the
unique partnership is as close as it ever was. You notice it
wherever they are – on the practice rink, in the press conferences where they speak as if with one mind. Most of all, however, you notice it when they perform. As soon as the music
starts to play they are not two individuals, but a single move-
ment, blending into each other, flowing, fluid, in unison.

Physically, they are ideal – Jayne is little more than a hundred pounds and small and Chris close to six feet tall, slen-
der but powerful about the shoulders, able to twist and turn
her, lift and launch her on a sheet of sheer ice with an
effortless ease that defies belief.

The data does not exist that could find and match two

**MACK AND
MABEL
REVISITED**
When we turned pro-
fessional, we were con-
stantly asked to
perform routines that
we did as amateur
competitors

A TORVILL AND DEAN CLASSIC For the original set pattern section in 1982 we did a blues to Larry Adler's haunting rendition of *Summertime*.

people so compatible as partners, and yet, in a city no bigger than Nottingham, chance brought them together when an instructor trying to place Chris with another girl came across Jayne's name as a skater who was unattached. Nothing before then had directed them towards each other. Chris was a successful ice dancer as a teenager and had another partner. Jayne had never even considered ice dancing, preferring the more acrobatic discipline of pairs skating, for which her smallness was a distinct advantage, and she had been a British junior champion.

Yet early one morning, at the invitation of an instructor at the Nottingham rink and so early in the day that Jayne admits having been bleary so with sleep that she can remember little of it, there began a partnership that was blessed. How else can you explain why the phone call that was to team them with Betty Callaway, their trainer, came to be made right when she was contemplating a letter announcing the retirement of another couple she trained, a letter that turned out to have been a misunderstanding? She was the catalyst of the team that gathered around Torvill and Dean, people like Courtney Jones, a former world champion ice dancer, and Bobby Thompson, a trainer. Each had an understanding of ice dancing and the ability to enhance Chris's creativity as a choreographer.

So many more contributed – dressmakers, ballet dancers, musicians, arrangers. Their parents, certainly, and Debbie Turner, an admirer who became their faithful personal assistant, smoothing their professional path and clearing the way for their return to amateur sport. All have played a part, and Jayne and Chris played theirs. For all of them, and their audiences, it has been a fantastic adventure. This is its story.

CHAPTER ONE

1975-81

E·A·R·L·Y

Y·E·A·R·S

The working partnership that became the most famous in ice skating began at the Thursday evening dance class at Nottingham Ice Rink, and not auspiciously. If any who were there now say that they saw what might one day be, their memory deceives them: Jayne fell in a blues number, hitting her head and elbow.

It was hardly surprising. A pairs skater who had tasted success, she competed at the European Championships at the age of fourteen. She had tried ice dancing years earlier but long forgotten the steps she was taught, and there were many she had never learned. She was there only because Chris and his partner, with whom he had won the British

Primary Championships, had a falling out. Jayne might not have been the obvious choice, but having lost her pairs partner to another girl, she was unattached – and willing.

Janet Sawbridge, a former British champion at both pairs and dance and a new instructor at Nottingham, sized them up, liked what she found and put them together. Under her teaching, they developed so well in four months that in their first competition together they were second.

Those who knew them say that they were a shy pair, but they lived close to each other, she above her parents' newsagent's shop and he a few streets away. They became friends and their partnership evolved. A local competition at Sheffield brought them their first victory, and eleven months after teaming up they became Northern champions.

Their skating now occupied every spare hour – two hours every day, sometimes four, and always three hours on Sundays. But there were failures on the way. The first time they took the National Skating Association's test, which would qualify them to compete in the National Championships, Chris

JAYNE MIGHT NOT HAVE BEEN THE OBVIOUS CHOICE, BUT WAS UNATTACHED – AND WILLING.

failed. They passed after a second attempt, but the partnership was strained by other demands. Chris, a police cadet, had to attend a police college in Yorkshire. He could train only at weekends, and the double life was tiring him. More than once he told Jayne to find another partner, but she would not hear of it, fetching him before dawn and driving from places up to forty-five minutes away to keep him in training.

Her perseverance paid off. They won their first international competition in St Gervais, Switzerland, and their second in Oberstdorf, an Alpine resort in Bavaria that was to become their training base. In 1977 they won selection for the 1978 European and World Championships. They were on the main highway to success, but the journey's destination was far from view: they were ninth at the Europeans, eleventh at the Worlds.

THEY WON THEIR FIRST INTERNATIONAL COMPETITION IN ST GERVAIS.

Not everything went smoothly. On their return from the World Championships they learned that Janet Sawbridge was expecting a baby and had decided to give up teaching. They would have to find a new trainer.

Many were considered, but all were too far from Nottingham, where Chris was tied to his police duties and Jayne to a job in insurance. Then the manager of the Nottingham rink suggested Betty Callaway, a former professional skater who had trained a German couple to the European title and was helping a Hungarian couple, Krisztina Regoeczy and Andras Sallay. He made contact with her, put the question, and the timing turned out to be perfect.

Callaway had received a letter from Hungary that she understood to mean that Regoeczy and Sallay were retiring. Free of commitments – she thought – she agreed to spend each weekend with Torvill and Dean at Nottingham for little more than her expenses. They would be her first British couple. It would be an interesting challenge. Then came the news that the Hungarians never intended to retire. The

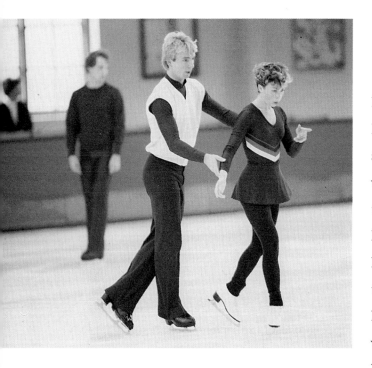

NOTTINGHAM ICE RINK
Nottingham Ice Rink was our first home, where one early morning we were brought together as ice dancers. But the hours when we could use the rink were uncivilized, the ice often crowded, and as soon as we climbed a few rungs on the ladder we sought sanctuary in quieter rinks in Switzerland and Germany.

letter had been misinterpreted, but Betty refused to go back on her agreement, and a deal was agreed whereby the Hungarians would train on weekdays with Betty in Richmond, where they would be her priority, and at weekends all three would commute to Nottingham to join Chris and Jayne. It worked. Both couples were to become world champions.

The winter of 1979/80 Jayne and Chris improved to sixth in the European Championships and eighth in the Worlds. They were making strides and becoming noticed. Advice was offered and accepted from many wishing to see them succeed. Lawrence Demmy suggested to Betty that Jayne should project herself more, change her hairstyle and wear less subtle make-up. Zoltan Nagy, a Hungarian ballet dancer who accompanied Regoeczy and Sallay abroad, helped Chris on his moves, and their choice of routines and music matured.

There are three elements in ice-dancing competition: compulsory dances, comprising two sections in which each couple perform the same routine to the same music — such as blues, paso doble or rumba — are the least rewarding both to the skaters and their marks. Betty was acknowledged mistress of these. In the second, skaters choose their own music and original dance to a specified rhythm. In the finale there is a free choice of music, rhythm and routine, so originality and creativity are important — Chris's forte.

For the 1980/81 season, he chose *On a Little Street in Singapore* for their original dance, a foxtrot, and introduced jazz to ice dancing with a combination of Glen Miller's *In the Mood* and Benny Goodman's *Swing, Swing, Swing*. The judges approved. At the European Championships in Gothenburg they were awarded eleven marks of 5.7 and finished fourth. At the Winter Olympic Games in Lake Placid they were fifth and were back to fourth at the World Championships.

Their accession came sooner than expected: the next winter. Both were totally committed now, having given up their jobs, and they were dependent on a generous yearly grant of £14,000 from Nottingham City Council. It paid early dividends.

For that season they chose *Cherry Pink and Apple Blossom White* for the required cha-cha original, and a selection with a rock-'n'-roll flavour for the free. It was their compulsories, however, that sent them on course for their dramatic first victory in February 1981 at the European Championships in Innsbruck — they were first in all. They stayed first after the original, but narrowly; the free would be decisive. Immediately behind them were the new Olympic champions and a couple who were formerly world champions. Torvill and Dean had to be at their best, and they were. Seven of the nine judges placed them first.

Four weeks later they were world champions. All nine judges placed them first after the original dance, all nine awarded them 5.9 for their free programme. The succession had been decided, the new king and queen of ice dance crowned.

IN THE MOOD

For our first Olympic season, we took jazz as our theme – Glenn Miller's *In the Mood* and Benny Goodman's *Swing, Swing, Swing* – it worked for us immediately. When we debuted in London, we were able to beat our Hungarian training partners, Krisztina Regoeczy and Andras Sallay, who also worked with Betty Callaway and who became world champions later that season. We were satisfied by our improvement to fifth place at the Olympics at Lake Placid, but the main jubilation in the British camp was over the victory of the Bristol figure skater Robin Cousins in the men's event.

THE WESTMINSTER WALTZ

The Westminster Waltz at the 1981 European Championships in Innsbruck, the first of four compulsory dances there, was a milestone for us. For the first time the judges placed us number one, ahead of the previous year's Olympic champions. We were surprised by the results because three of the couples ahead of us the year before were still competing. We stayed first after a paso doble, rumba and cha-cha, and over the next four years of competition we always managed to be first in compulsories.

WORLD CHAMPIONS FOR THE FIRST TIME

We won our first European and World titles in 1981 to a routine that began with jazz music from *Fame*, changed into an Eygptian theme with *Caravan*, slowed to a seductive rumba from *Red Sails in the Sunset* and finished with *Swing, Swing, Swing*. It was the last time we stitched music together in that fashion but it worked. Seven of the nine judges at the Europeans placed us first and an eighth first equal. Only one Russian judge voted for a Russian couple, Irina Moiseyeva and Andrei Minenko, former world champions. A few weeks later, in Hartford, Connecticut, our marks rose higher, the Russians slipped, and we became world champions for the first time.

CHAPTER TWO

1982

M·A·C·K

A·N·D

M·A·B·E·L

Torvill and Dean were world champions now, but for how long? The old order had been swept away, but there were new challengers appearing from the Soviet Union and the United States. Many, even among their British admirers, feared that they had peaked too early in the four-year cycle that leads to the ultimate competition, the Olympic Games.

Each season demands something fresh – new costumes, new music, new routines – and if they were to defend the reputation established in 1981, they had to be different. What to do next was a thought even before the last season had ended.

As so often, they found the answer in an idea that had occurred to them as a possibility years earlier

I WON'T SEND ROSES
(Preceding pages) We performed a special section of Mack and Mabel at the Richmond gala in 1982. This is the final pose.

ACCOLADES
We were proud to receive a number of honours after the triumphs of 1981. Prime Minister Margaret Thatcher attended a gala in Richmond, and she invited us to 10 Downing Street. The city council in our home town of Nottingham, which supported us financially, also conferred on us the freedom of the city.

and been consigned to the back of their minds. In one of their periodic visits to the library of their local radio station in Nottingham, they found a recording of a Broadway show. Called *Mack and Mabel*, the show had been a flop, closing after nine days. But they liked its overture, and Chris saw possibilities in the melodramatic story of a love affair between the silent-movie star Mack Sennett and his leading lady, Mabel Normand.

Most free dances are a potpourri of music spliced together to give four minutes of various styles and tempos. Chris had it in his mind to offer a single piece telling a whole story, lifted almost intact from the overture. Ice dancing had never seen its like, and it might have challenged the natural conservatism of the judges, but Chris set about creating a cameo that would tell of a dramatic love affair through to its climactic ending.

The other choice to be made was the original dance. The International Skating Union had dictated that it should be a blues that season, and that brought to their mind an edition of a chat show in which Larry Adler performed on his harmonica the old Gershwin standard, *Summertime*. The ISU's rules allow a range of tempos, and Chris chose the slowest, emphasizing its sombre, haunting appeal to create a soulful routine.

The work on both was done in Oberstdorf. Sometimes

Betty would be with them, and they went for help on perfecting the dances to Michael Stylianos, a former Latin
American ballroom world champion whose advice they had
sought on their cha-cha the previous year. But the dances
remained their own creation, every step calculated and polished to their own rising standards. Some steps followed a
natural progression; others
offered themselves by chance.
The scissor steps in Mack and
Mabel, which were to become
famous, came about when they
were playing around without

**EVERY STEP WAS CALCULATED
AND POLISHED TO THEIR
OWN RISING STANDARDS.**

the music, unable to synchronize their steps. In the mirror
they happened to catch the effect of the move, and it was
incorporated into the piece.

There were other innovations. One was an unusual move
in which Chris lifted Jayne under her shoulder blades and
twisted her to bring them face to face before returning her
to the ice. Another had Jayne throwing herself on Chris's
hip, from which he twirled her horizontally. The ice-dancing
world was to see a revolution, but would it be welcome?

The public premiere of the new routine was at an event at
the Richmond rink in west London. There were none of the
potential international challengers to beat, but its reception
by the audience as well as the judges was crucial. Word can
spread quickly in the small world of ice dancing, and judges
can be influenced by good reports from others. They could
not have hoped for more than they were to receive that
evening. Summertime received one six, an uncommon mark

for an original dance, and Mack and Mabel won sixes from a Canadian, an Austrian and, significantly, a Russian judge.

The next test was the British Championships at their home rink in Nottingham, which presented a special kind of pressure. There was no doubt that they would win; there were only six competitors. But how comfortably?

They need not have worried. Sixes were becoming the hallmark of their performances. All nine judges awarded them sixes for artistic impression, and seven of them the maximum score again for technical merit. The reaction, at the rink and from the audience on television, was ecstatic.

Suddenly, Torvill and Dean were more popular in Britain than their sport. The country was going through a difficult time economically, and they lifted everyone's spirits. They were British and the best. A week later, when they took the National Skating Association's gold-star test, normally a private occasion attended only by judges and the press, a thousand spectators greeted them.

SIXES WERE BECOMING THE HALLMARK OF THEIR PERFORMANCES.

The European Championships in Lyon, France, followed, and again Torvill and Dean triumphed. The judges seemed convinced that here was a couple who could raise the discipline to greater heights, and they fell over each other to heap the honours upon them. They were marked first by every judge on each compulsory dance, with second places going to a Russian couple, Natalia Bestemianova and Andre Bukin. Summertime confirmed their preeminence, and the French crowd broke into applause that threatened to drown the music on their final circuit. All around the rink people were in tears of emotion, and their reward was three pairs of sixes, the perfect score of twelve.

It was not over yet. The Russians could still win by taking the free programme, and they drew to skate first. They scored six 5.9s and nothing below 5.7, but it was a hopeless task because the judges held back, leaving room on their scorecards for what they knew was to come. Jayne and Chris got three sixes for technical merit and eight for artistic impression, a total of eleven – and a record at the time for an international championship.

ALL AROUND THE RINK PEOPLE WERE IN TEARS OF EMOTION.

At the World Championships in Copenhagen, they skated Summertime even better, the best ever, they both believe. This time they were awarded six sixes, and after Mack and Mabel the Brondby-Hallen rink was a field of flowers. They were world champions again, and for years ice dancing would not be the same. They had changed its character. Bernard Ford, a former world champion, put it perfectly: 'It's like watching God skate.'

MEN WITH TEARS

If our victory at the 1981 World Championships
surprised the world of ice dancing, Mack and
Mabel, our free dance, must have seemed revo-
lutionary. But it was our programme for
Summertime that set the tone. After we skated it
at the 1982 European Championships in Lyon,
we were told that there were men watching with
tears in their eyes.

SIXES ON AN ORIGINAL DANCE

At the European Championships we received three sixes for artistic impression, the first we'd been awarded for an original dance, but the record lasted only a few weeks: at the World Championships, six judges awarded us sixes for artistic impression. A French woman liked it enough to give us a six twice, a first for an original dance.

A ROMANCE OF PURE MELODRAMA
Mack and Mabel was the story of the silent-movie
star Mack Sennett and the stormy love affair with
his leading lady, Mabel Normand. Chris took the
music from the overture to the Broadway show
and wove around it a romance of pure melodrama: the tale of a rejected woman tossed away by
her man and her attempts to win him back.

CHANGING TEMPO
We used all four minutes allowed for our free
programme, which in itself started a trend in the
sport. Here Jayne has thrown herself backwards
onto Chris's knee, signalling a change in the
piece's tempo.

PURE GOLD

Though Mack and Mabel bombed on stage, it created history on ice for us. Part of its success were our matching eye-catching gold costumes, a one-button gold tuxedo with bow tie for Chris and a simple dress adorned by feathers for Jayne. At the World Championships in Copenhagen we had a near disaster when Chris's tuxedo button came unbuttoned and threatened to interfere with the routine.

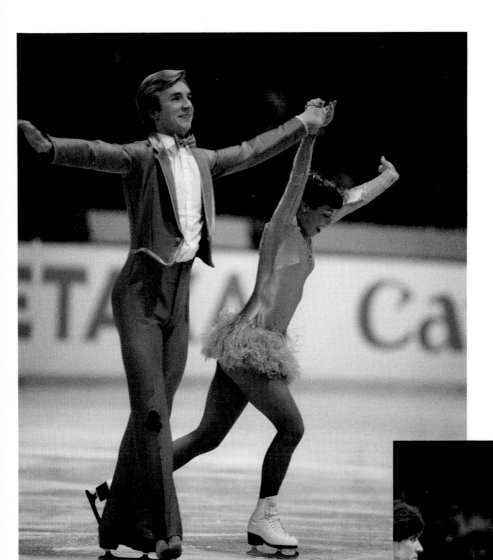

AN AVALANCHE OF BOUQUETS
When we finished Mack and Mabel at the European Championships in Lyons, there was an avalanche of bouquets, ovations and sixes – eleven out of a possible eighteen.

AN EYE FOR FASHION
It was Courtney Jones, a former world ice dance champion and friend, who came up with the costume design. He used to skate around the practice rink behind us holding a tailor's chalk to make adjustments to the line and fitting. Detail was important to us, so everyone around us paid attention to every aspect of our performances.

CHAPTER THREE

1983

B★A★R★N★U★M

After every World Championship, the International
Skating Union invites the champions and other
medallists on a world tour. It is hard work for little
reward, but it is expected as a gesture to the sport.
In 1982, though, it offered Jayne and Chris an
unexpected bonus.

On a trip to Moscow for three days, some of the
skaters were given tickets to the Bolshoi Ballet for
one free evening. Chris was among them, and since
ballet was a great love of his, he would normally
have jumped at the chance. Instead, he had his
mind set on something else, and he exchanged his
ticket with a Canadian skater who had been invited
to the Moscow State Circus.

There was a good reason. He was already thinking ahead to the next great challenge, and the circus had occurred to him as a possibility, full as it was of so many different movements, jugglers, trapeze artists, clowns and the music. The idea grew on him when he picked up a tape of Barnum, then a hit on Broadway and in London's West End. It happened to be a French-language version, but what mattered was the music and its appeal. Immediately he booked tickets for the show at the London Palladium for Jayne and himself.

They were recognized faces now, and spotted in the audience by the show's star, Michael Crawford, they were invited backstage. Could they use the music for their next routine, they asked. No problem, he said. But there was: vocals are banned from ice dancing, and there was no purely orchestral recording. Crawford came up with the solution, recruiting Michael Reed, the show's musical director. He put the music to piano, then brought musicians into a studio to record the full work – the first time music had been recorded to ice dancers' own specifications. They were leading the way once again.

Their original dance that year was rock 'n' roll. Again they happened upon an idea for the routine while sitting in a theatre. This time they were watching Andrew Lloyd Webber's *Song and Dance,*

OBERSTDORF
Not a fall on the ice but a roll in the snow. The work of creating and perfecting our routines was done each autumn in the Bavarian town of Oberstdorf, a place where we could relax away from the pressure of public and media attention at home. We chose it originally because the Nottingham rink closed for repairs at a critical time in our preparation, but the benefits of Oberstdorf drew us back year after year.

near the end of which the ballet dancer Wayne Sleep per-
forms a rock sequence based on the music of Paganini. It
was different. They seized on it.

The problem then became keeping the new dance and,
more importantly, Barnum to themselves. Everybody now
waited on them. What Torvill
and Dean would do as an
encore to last year's triumphs
was a subject of concern to
their competitors and of great
interest to the British public.

**THEY KEPT THE ROUTINE
UNDER WRAPS, AND THE
EVENING OF THE EVENT WAS
HEAVY WITH EXPECTATION.**

Revealed too soon it would lose its impact, a point that Chris
always bore in mind as inveterate showman. So that winter
they declined invitations to compete in the season's events,
agreeing only to skate an exhibition at a London gala in
which the audience had to be content with a reprise of Mack
and Mabel. Only on the eve of the British Championships in
Nottingham, at a press conference indicative of the public
interest they now aroused, did they reveal their plan. Even
the London correspondent of a Moscow newspaper
appeared.

The story of Crawford's close involvement was told, but he
was still one of the few who had actually seen the work performed. Even at the final official practice in Nottingham
with judges present they kept it under wraps, and the
evening of the event was heavy with expectation.

First, though, came the original. They wore simple white T-
shirts, adorned only with the initials CJ, she with a black
dress underneath and he with black trousers, both wearing a

red scarf around their necks. They were rewarded for the dance with two sixes.

What followed was altogether different, a hilarious interpretation of a full circus show, with tightrope walking, clowning and a marching band. Both were in shiny white, accented by bright blue sashes and facings, and in an instant the ice rink became a sawdust ring, and everybody was transported into the Big Top. It was fun, it was clever, and it was a winner. A small trip flawed it, but every mark was 5.9 except a single six.

Incredibly, they were unhappy with the performance. Revisions were made – a more daring lift was added and a cartwheel dropped – and while practising the lift Jayne fell badly on her side and shoulder. No bones were broken but she was off the ice for days, and when she returned she fell again on the same lift. Hardly able to move her arm now, she was forced to withdraw them from the forthcoming European Championships.

Not until two weeks before the World Championships in Helsinki were they able to practise their routines again in full, and even then they avoided the more energetic sections of the rock 'n' roll dance to safeguard Jayne's arm. Betty, however, revealed that she knew two weeks before Helsinki that they were ready. 'On this occasion they could do no wrong', she recalled. 'It was perfect, perfect. I don't think that Chris and Jayne even took one breath that was slightly different to the other's.'

IT WAS FUN, IT WAS CLEVER, AND IT WAS A WINNER.

They were as good as new once the competition began. An unprecedented row of 5.9s for one compulsory greeted their return, even though Jayne was skating with strapping around her shoulder, evident beneath her T-shirt when they performed the rock 'n' roll. But if the bandage affected her, it did not detract from her performance, and the judges bestowed fresh honours – another seven sixes.

Nothing prepared the Finnish audience for what was to come next. They skated Barnum to perfection. The crowd stood to them as one, showering the ice with bouquets and toys. Nine 5.9s for technical merit flashed first onto the scoreboard, followed immediately by nine sixes. Jayne let loose an ear-splitting shriek of excitement; beside them, Crawford punched the air.

Over the three sections of the competition – the compulsories, original and free – they averaged a mark of slightly more than 5.9. Sport had never come so close to being perfectly performed, and those of us fortunate enough to be present felt we were seeing one of the great moments in sporting history. What we could not have known – and would probably have refused to believe – was that there was better to come. We could not have comprehended it on that wonderful night in Helsinki.

THREE MINDS, ONE THOUGHT
At the practice rink in Oberstdorf, our trainer Betty Callaway talks over the morning's workout. Continually looking for improvement, we were never satisfied with what we had – we were always evolving.

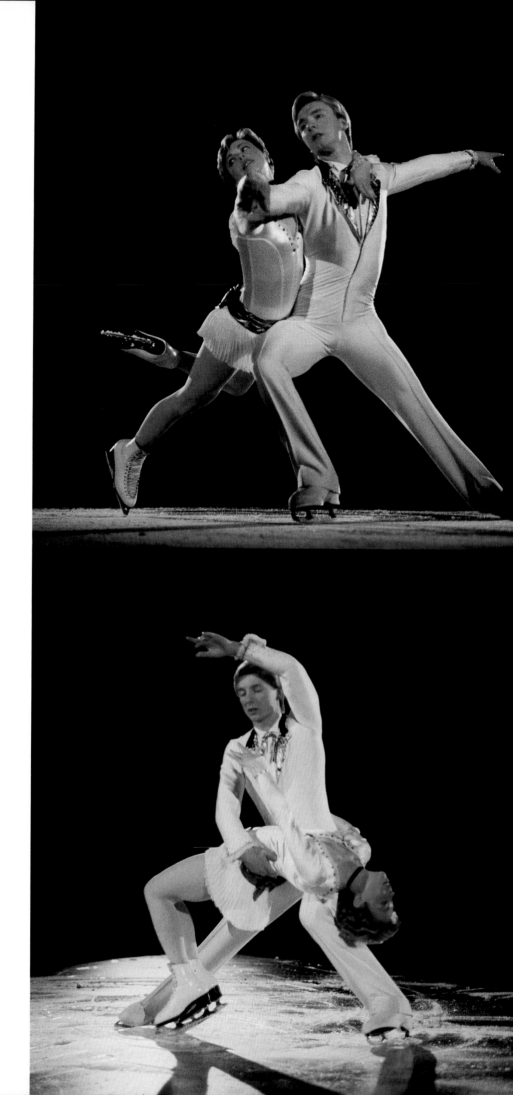

GOLD INTO WHITE
After the gold costumes of
Mack and Mabel, we chose
the simplicity of white for
the circus act we devised
for Barnum, our free
dance for 1983. Sparkling
blue lapels and a cravat on
Chris and a sash around
Jayne's waist highlighted
the effect.

AN EMBRACE IN HELSINKI

Skating from the ice, the first bouquet and toy animal thrown on the ice already in our hands. After Barnum all nine judges at the World Championships in Helsinki awarded us sixes for artistic impression, a decision that earned a standing ovation for the judges as much as for us.

TRAPEZE ARTISTS ON ICE

The Barnum routine ran through the gamut of the circus, the trapeze artists, the clowns and the trombones of the band. In this scene Chris lifts Jayne in preparation for swinging her into a head over heels. Rival coaches questioned at the time whether it was within the rules, but the judges unanimously endorsed its legality.

KISS ME KATE

(Following pages) We performed *Kiss Me Kate* at a blues exhibition.

CHAPTER FOUR

1 9 8 4

B•O•L•E•R•O

All that had gone before had in many ways been preparation for the Olympic Games, sport's ultimate challenge, so that all that they had achieved until now meant very little. Everything had to be new; only their reputation would go before them.

Twice they had worked their magic with a story. The audience was coming to expect it, but to try it a third time might be thought clichéd. They chose instead to create a mood using Ravel's *Bolero* and to take its slow crescendo to a dramatic conclusion. There was a thin story behind it, that of two lovers who could not live together but refused to be apart, leading them on a journey up a mountain from which they would hurl themselves to their

VICTORY AT THE EUROPEAN CHAMPIONSHIPS
Bolero was still to come, but Jayne is almost in tears and Chris is
exultant as the judges award us six perfect sixes for artistic impression. We were disappointed that the Russian judge gave us only
5.6 for technique and placed us second behind our main challengers, the Soviet couple Natalya Bestemianova and Andrei
Bukin. But the other skaters were more generous. Bestemianova
even said that she could not free our performance from her
thoughts for the rest of that day – and that is one of the highest
compliments we could get.

deaths in a suicide pact. It was the beauty of the piece, the intensity of the emotion and the breathtaking finale as they threw themselves to the ice that grabbed the heart. The mysticism of Ravel's seventeen-minute composition was squeezed into four.

Half the world now seemed interested only in knowing whether they were as close off the ice as they appeared to be on it. Could any two people of the opposite sex look so deeply into each other's eyes with such fervour then just switch off at the rinkside? It was, says Jayne now, all a performance, play-acting, assuming a role and becoming it for four minutes – like any good actor does. 'We are making love for two minutes on the ice, and then we are just good friends', she was to say more recently of a blues dance.

But the public and media wanted more. Journalists beat a path to their training camp in Oberstdorf throughout the autumn of 1983 in pursuit of secret knowledge. Oh, yes, the ice dancing is all very interesting, they would say, but what about it? Can we hear wedding bells? All Jayne and Chris could think about was their one last lap of sporting honour. It looks so effortless, so serene, when it is performed but behind the aesthetic excellence are bruises, sweat and at times not a few tears.

EVEN THE SHARPNESS OF THEIR SKATES WAS CRITICAL, A FEW HUNDREDTHS OF A CENTIMETRE DIFFERENCE WAS DETECTABLE.

Their attention to detail could wreck a computer. Nothing can be left to chance. Jayne flew from Oberstdorf to London to get a piece of music right. Their costumer designer, Courtney Jones, skated behind them on the ice before sewing extra stitches into a blouse to improve its effect. Even the sharpness of their skates was critical, a few hundredths of a centimetre difference detectable when they skate at the limits.

But first came the choreography. The ISU chose a paso doble as the original for 1984 and threatened themselves with an avalanche of Españas. Chris and Jayne decided to take a bull-fighting theme in which Jayne would be the cape, he the matador, and to capture the feeling Jones came up with a costume that some consider his greatest creation.

It was Bolero, however, that caused controversy. There were lifts in it according to a Russian coach, Titiana Tarassova, which broke the rule that the man's hand should not be raised above shoulder height. Not so, said Lawrence Demmy, chairman of the ISU's ice-dancing committee, adding sarcastically: 'I'm delighted to hear that after all these years the Russians have found their rule book.'

A few weeks before the Olympic Games, at the European Championships in Budapest, the Russians were still arguing the toss. Alexander Gorshkov, a former world champion, and the Russian judge Irina Absaliamova claimed that there were also faults in Torvill and Dean's original dance. When it came to marking it, Absaliamova gave it only 5.6 for technical merit, confirming that she believed something to be amiss with it.

She was spitting into the wind of change sweeping through ice dancing. It had long been the poor relation of figure skating, only arriving as an Olympic sport in 1976, and those concerned with its future well-being were not going to let a stone-hearted traditionalist spoil its most glorious hour. They were all in T & D's train, falling over themselves to set new records. In Budapest the two even achieved their ambition to score a six in a compulsory outside of Britain – and not just one. For their Westminster Waltz, three could find no fault with it, a mark never before awarded in an international championship. They were to do it again with the same dance at the Olympics.

IN BUDAPEST THE TWO EVEN ACHIEVED THEIR AMBITION TO SCORE A SIX IN A COMPULSORY – AND NOT JUST ONE.

When it came to Bolero, even Mrs Absaliamova's heart was touched. She was among all but one of the judges who gave it the stamp of artistic approval with sixes. The Britons regained the European title loaned temporarily a year earlier because of their enforced absence.

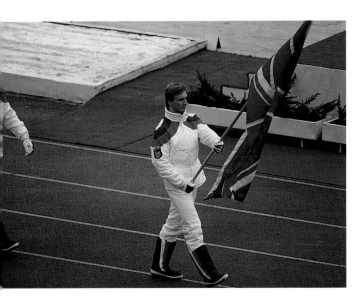

BRITISH HOPES
The first Olympic honour for Chris. He was chosen by the British team leaders to carry the flag at the opening ceremony of the 1984 Winter Games in Sarajevo, recognition that the British had hopes of a gold medal for us. Since we had won the European title against our principal rivals from the Soviet Union, interest focussed more on whether we would win even more sixes with Bolero than we did with Barnum.

So to Sarajevo. They trained for it in Oberstdorf and made their way in private to the games by train. Awaiting them was in full splendour the world's media, press conferences, photo opportunities, endless questions. But the only one that mattered was answered in the Zetra Stadium.

A formidable margin was put between them and the Russians in the compulsories, and increased when Torvill and Dean picked up four sixes in the original. Bolero did the rest. It was pure theatre. When they fell to the ice at the finish, the audience stood cheering for so long it was as though they were demanding an encore. Three sixes and six 5.9s for technical merit. Nine sixes for artistic impression – artistic perfection would be fairer. The gold, the Olympic title, was theirs.

It should have ended there, but they went through the motions of winning their fourth world title in Ottawa, Canada, the following month. Nobody remembers the 1984 World Championships now (except that the ice-machine broke down and kept television viewers wanting to see the performace live awake until the early hours of the morning). All that is forged in the memory is that single magnificent performance in Sarajevo.

THE BULLFIGHT

The paso doble was nominated for the original dance in the Olympic season, and we elected to present a scene from a bullfight: Chris was the matador, Jayne the cape. Her costume was a black cape with a gold fringe along the arms. When she spread out her arms, she revealed a flash of white from wrist to waist, like a cape being held in front of a bull. Though the choreography was planned first, the way Jayne's costume opened began to dictate changes that Chris would use to best effect.

THE PASO DOBLE

The conventional rhythm was 4/4 time, but we wanted to be different, so we decided to put a piece by Rimsky-Korsakov to 6/8 beat, a challenging task for a routine that had to be doubly squeezed into the two minutes allowed by the rules. We found Robert Stewart, a music teacher at a school in Surrey who conducted a church choir and had a background in the commercial musical world. We persuaded him to produce a score that turned out to be outstanding.

THE JOURNEY UP THE MOUNTAIN

The routine was the story of two lovers who have found each other but who know they cannot be together. So as one they climb a mountain, represented by the rising power of the music, until they reach the top and die together by throwing themselves off, a climax portrayed by a dramatic fall. We think it was perhaps the first time that a fall had been built into a skating programme.

FOUR MINUTES OF BOLERO

A sequence from Bolero, and this is just for
starters. Ravel's music in full takes seven-
teen minutes to build its great crescendo,
but the rules of ice dancing permitted us
only four minutes. Incredibly, Robert
Stewart managed to make the cuts without
losing the effect, but to emphasize the climactic end the start had to be slow. Chris
leans to take Jayne by the ankle and turn
her over onto her skates. She turns, plead-
ing with him to follow, finally bringing him
to his feet as she skates away. We hoped the
routine would be seen as a journey.

71

**A PERFECT ROW
OF SIXES**
Bolero was a fitting
finale to our amateur
career. It is claimed
that 100 million view-
ers around the world
watched us in Sara-
jevo. We're glad we
could leave behind
perfect sixes – and a
world record for ice
skating at the Olympic
Games.

CHAPTER FIVE

1 9 8 5 - 9 3

T•O•U•R•I•N•G

T•H•E

G•L•O•B•E

It was time to move on. Nothing could quite follow Bolero on a sporting stage, and it was best that they did not try. There were fresh pastures, new challenges, and they lay in the commercial world. It was time for Chris to cast off the chains of competition and let his creativity run riot. There was a living to be made, but it was the prize of artistic freedom that appealed, and even before the Olympic season they were bursting to expand their horizons.

First stops on their professional tour were Australia and New Zealand. They toured with a group of Russian skaters, among whom were several who had competed against them. They appeared at the Royal Variety Performance in London.

WITHOUT RULES
Wherever we performed, audiences liked to see our most famous numbers. We must have been asked to do Bolero a thousand times. Our first professional tour with our own company of international skaters gave us the licence to delve deeper into our creative resources. We came up with a succession of new show-stopping numbers, seen by British fans when the tour called at Wembley Arena in London, for which we had a specially commissioned Big Top tent for the event. We performed the beautiful Song of India (above) and Shepard's Song (preceding pages).

Sport did not forget them immediately. At the year's end BBC Television's viewers voted them Sports Personalities of the Year (they had been Team of the Year in 1983), and they won their first professional world ice-dance championship in America, an event that did not demand rigorous training of compulsories and a victory that they repeated a year later.

Most of their time was taken up with touring in commerical shows and preparing routines for tours. 'Not just four minutes now but forty minutes at a time, sometimes eight times a week', said Chris. In 1985 they put together their own company of skaters for a world tour, something they were to repeat in 1988 on a grand scale with a company from the Soviet Union. Other companies, like the American Ice-Capades, called on their services, and there were television's demands to be satisfied. A brilliant production in 1986 called *Fire and Ice* was filmed for showing at Christmas in Britain.

Eventually the British television arts programme Omnibus, usually devoted to more obvious cultures, bestowed its approval on them with a documentary on Torvill and Dean choreography, proving at least that they had not lost their ability to win a television audience: it attracted the highest viewing figures for the programme that season. In 1990 they tested the sporting waters again, winning the world professional title and being chosen as world professional skaters of

THEY KNEW THAT AFTER TEN LONG YEARS THERE WOULD BE AN ENCORE TO BOLERO – THE 1994 OLYMPIC GAMES

the year. Chris began to choreograph competition pieces for a French-Canadian couple, Paul and Isabelle Duschenay, who went on to win the world title in 1991 and the silver medal at the 1992 Olympic Games.

In 1992 Torvill and Dean prepared a new show for a tour of Britain with a company of skaters recruited in the Ukraine. Weeks were spent in Kiev practising, and during the tour a television recording of it put the couple back on British television at Christmas. But by then, life for them had moved on. Sport was beckoning them back, and this time as competitors. When they skated Bolero again at a unique gathering of past Olympic champions in Boston, they knew that after ten long years there would be an encore – the 1994 Olympic Games.

THE WORLD TOUR

We were often asked to perform routines that we had had so much success with in amateur competition. With the atmospheric lighting available to us on the professional tour, we were able to take dances like Mack and Mabel to new heights. In addition to England, our 1985 tour called on Australia, New Zealand, Canada and the United States.

TILT

We were delighted when the television programme Omnibus wanted to do a documentary on our choreography. The music for Tilt was a collaboration between English jazz saxophonist Andy Sheppard and Chris, and it allowed us to explore a whole new direction.

WORKING IN KIEV

Our last commercial show toured Britain in 1992 with a company of Ukrainian dancers. All the preparations and rehearsals were done in Kiev. Andris Toppe, a former Latvian ballet dancer who is naturalized Australian, was rehearsal director and choreographer. Among the dances featuring the company were Over the Rainbow (below), Skaters' Waltz and Hoedown (right) – a Counry and Western Torvill and Dean style. Our rehearsal spaces (following pages) often showed signs of the former Soviet Union.

CHAPTER SIX

1994

L·E·T'·S
F·A·C·E T·H·E
M·U·S·I·C
A·N·D D·A·N·C·E

Chance brought them back into the sporting arena, just as it had brought them together all those years before in Nottingham. This time the invitation was to attend the one hundredth anniversary celebration of the International Skating Union in Davos, Switzerland. Many of their old friends were there – the officials, judges and skaters of their earlier years – and the atmosphere was right. They learned that the ISU was changing its rule on the eligibility of skaters and professionals would be welcome for the first time.

Chris was interested. On the train journey from Davos, he mentioned it to Jayne. 'I thought he was drunk, or something', she recalled. But the idea of

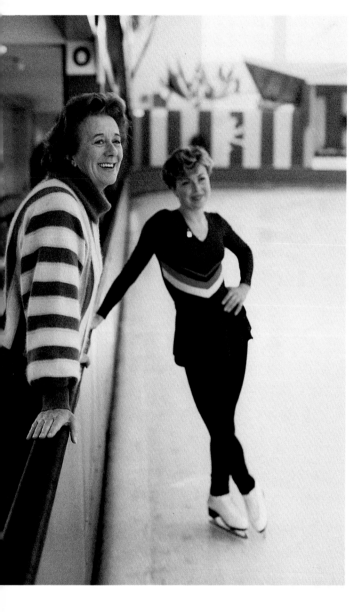

PASSING THE TORCH
An old picture of Jayne and Betty Callaway, who says that one day Jayne will make an excellent teacher. Already she has helped Betty with the training of Britain's most promising young couple, Justin Lanning and Marika Humphreys, and soon it may be Jayne on the other side of the boards.

one more competitive challenge grew until it became irresistible. Ten months later their minds were made up, their diaries cleared and Betty Callaway, along with Bobby Thompson, were recruited again as coaches. Their eligibility was reinstated.

This time Jayne and Chris decided that they would prepare themselves at home. They accepted an offer of mornings to themselves at Bladerunner Arena in Milton Keynes. Four hours on weekdays and two hours on Sunday they were there. Their fitness, honed by the professional demands of performing up to eight shows a week, was in peak form, and having lifted Jayne as many as ninety times in an evening in their shows, Chris felt stronger than ten years earlier. It was the technique that had to be polished again. 'It was like getting out a rusty bike and pedalling it again', said Chris. 'It was a six-month slog.' There were other equally important details – not least a free dance different enough from Bolero so as not to be compared.

The choice was *Let's Face the Music and Dance*, a tune composed by Irving Berlin and made famous in a 1936 Hollywood movie starring the dance couple they most admired: Fred Astaire and Ginger Rogers. Chris choreographed a piece of ballroom dancing that was as far removed from the passion of Bolero as it was possible to imagine, full of highly complex steps that led the eye towards the ice. All that remained was to offer it to an audience, and they did on one Saturday afternoon in January 1994 in the Sheffield Arena at the British Championships.

There was very little doubt that they would win their seventh British title, but when the compulsories were complete, all doubt was gone. Their first marks in amateur competition since 1984 were not startling, but the free dance was like old times. All nine judges gave sixes for artistic impression.

They expected the judging at the European Championships in Copenhagen two weeks later to be less generous, but they were surprised to be placed third in the first compulsory, and joint second with Oksana Gritschuk and Eugny Platov behind Maya Usova and Alexandr Zhulin at the end of the first day.

A well-received rumba that earned them two sixes lifted them to joint first with Usova and Zhulin, but their free dance, fine-tuned since Sheffield – with a cartwheel and two lifts added – did not find favour. It was the two Russian couples and skating's curious scoring system that conspired inadvertently to hand them their fourth European title. After ten years the magic was still there, and the greatest ice dancers in the world headed toward Lillehammer and the challenge of the Winter Olympics.

REPLAY
We're happy to say that after all those years the British Championships in Sheffield felt like a replay of the 1984 Olympics.

FACING THE MUSIC – AGAIN

The opening to our free programme was an interpretation of Irving Berlin's music *Let's Face the Music and Dance*, which Fred Astaire and Ginger Rogers made famous in the 1936 film *Follow the Fleet*. The steps were the most complicated we'd ever attempted – and fast: we reckon that the number of steps in all of Bolero could fit in the first minute of this routine.

1 2 3 4 5 6 7 8 9

6.0 6.0 6.0 6.0 6.0 6.0 6.0 6.0 6.0

THE SEVENTH TIME

If we missed one step, we'd miss them all – they come so quickly. But luckily we missed none at all, and we were astonished with our seventh British Championship. We were delighted to be selected as Britain's representatives at the European Championships in Copenhagen.

STEPPING OUT
After the joy of victory at the European Championships (above) we performed the rumba and the final section of Let's Face the Music and Dance for a gala exhibition (left) before setting out for Lille-hammer, Norway, and the 1994 Winter Olympics.

COMPETITION RECORD

1976	1st Sheffield Trophy
	1st Northern championship
	1st St Gervais
	2nd Oberstdorf
	4th British championship
1977	1st Oberstdorf
	3rd British championship
1978	9th European championship, Strasbourg
	11th World championship, Ottawa
	1st John Davis Trophy
	1st British championship (first 6.0)
1979	6th European championship, Zagreb
	8th World Championship, Vienna
	2nd Rotary Watches competition, Richmond
	1st British Championship
	2nd NHK competition, Tokyo
1980	4th European championship, Gothenburg
	5th Olympic Games, Lake Placid
	4th World championship, Dortmund
	1st St Ivel competition, Richmond
	1st British championship
1981	1st European championship, Innsbruck
	1st World championship, Hartford
	1st St Ivel competition, Richmond
	1st British championship
1982	1st European championship, Lyons
	1st World championship, Copenhagen
	1st British championship
1983	1st World championship, Helsinki
1984	1st European championship
	1st Olympic Games, Sarajevo
	1st World championship, Helsinki
1994	1st British championship, Sheffield
	1st European championship, Copenhagen

First published in Great Britain in 1994 by

George Weidenfeld and Nicolson Ltd

The Orion Publishing Group

Orion House

5 Upper St Martin's Lane

London WC2H 9EA

Edited by Lucas Dietrich

Designed by Bradbury and Williams

Litho origination by Pixel Colour Ltd, London

Printed and bound by Butler & Tanner Ltd, Frome and London

A catalogue record for this book is available from the British
Library.

ISBN 0297 833 863